AF211876

MILES RIZZO

THE PROFITABLE CONTENT SYSTEM

The Ultimate Guide on How to Create and Repurpose Your Content, Discover the Best Ways on How to Make the Most Out Of Your Content

Descrierea CIP a Bibliotecii Naţionale a României
MILES RIZZO
  THE PROFITABLE CONTENT SYSTEM. The Ultimate
Guide on How to Create and Repurpose Your Content,
Discover the Best Ways on How to Make the Most Out Of Your
Content / Miles Rizzo – Bucharest: Editura My Ebook, 2021
  ISBN

MILES RIZZO

THE PROFITABLE CONTENT SYSTEM

The Ultimate Guide on How to Create and Repurpose Your Content, Discover the Best Ways on How to Make the Most Out Of Your Content

My Ebook Publishing House
Bucharest, 2021

CONTENTS

INTRODUCTION

How good are you at taking one piece of content and using it in several different ways? Or do you just buy private label rights (PLR) material, make a few changes to it and then post the content on your blog? If you are not reusing or repurposing your content you are not making the best use of your time.

This eBook will show you how to get the most out of each piece of your content, simply by using the same content in different ways. Once you begin to see how easy this is you will be kicking yourself for not doing this earlier.

Using the same content in slightly different ways and for various purposes will help you free up your time and will save you money in the long run. You won't have to constantly buy new content because you have become a pro at using one purchase multiple times.

The tips and pointers in this eBook pertain to material that you have written yourself and to any type of PLR or other material you may have purchased. These pointers will be an excellent way to differentiate your PLR from others and will enable you to make your content totally new and unique!

SIMPLE TIPS FOR CREATING POWERPOINT SLIDES

One of the easiest ways to get more use out of your content is by turning simple articles into PowerPoint slides. You can then use these slides for various purposes including slide shows and for creating videos.

If you are using Microsoft PowerPoint then you can choose from various styles of templates for your slides. Choose one that matches the topic of your article or you may wish to create a custom slide with your business logo on it.

Make use of free images and the clipart within Microsoft PowerPoint itself. See how you can take a plain paragraph and add visual elements to it to create something brand new. As well consider using different colored fonts in one or two sizes and styles. You definitely don't want to overdo the use of too many different fonts. Try to use them for adding impact and drawing attention to certain points within your article.

Add Your Title Here

Add article text in this section

>Use bullet points
>Colors and
> *Font Size & style*
>to visually enhance your
slides

Add website Logo here

As you can see it is very easy to add additional elements and dress up your plain articles. A 400 word article will give you about 10 to 12 slides which you can then use in various ways.

You don't have to use the entire article either. You may prefer to just take the highlights of each article and then feature them as bullet points on your slides.

When creating slides don't be afraid to resize the text boxes and play with the colors and font styles and sizes until you find ones that you are happy with.

Always look for free images or images that come with royalty free rights attached to them. These allow you to publish them in your content without any copyright infringements.

Great photographs can also be used as a background for your slides. Just make sure that the photograph is not too busy and that your text is easy to read.

Once you have your content saved as a PowerPoint presentation you still have additional options from here.

Open up Windows Movie Maker and turn your slides into a video. You can add a voice over or a sound track to your movie. Once you have created your video it can be uploaded to any of the video sharing sites. Just remember to add a slide that has your URL on it so people can visit your website.

Alternatively you can save your slides into a PDF and this creates a magazine style document. This is really effective if you use quality images inside. Don't forget about changing the page orientation in PowerPoint and using the portrait view. This works well if you have lots of text on each slide.

So far we have created:

- 1 original article
- 1 Powerpoint Presentation
- 1 Video
- 1 PDF presentation from the slides

Let's continue

From this same article we can now create blog posts and autoresponder messages or emails.

Simply divide your article into two or three portions and use them for your blog posts or email messages. The nice thing about this is that you can easily schedule out your blog posts in Wordpress.

Simply go to the Publish panel inside your Post page and expand the Publish immediately box.

Here you can change the date and time of the post and schedule out your content for weeks or

even months at a time. A great job for a VA to do!

To add as content inside your autoresponder account you would just log in to your account and then select the appropriate list. Below is a screenshot of how you would do this inside your Aweber account.

Create a new message and then simply copy and paste the portion of the article you want to use into your new message.

Schedule your messages to go out weekly or every three to four days. Repeat until you have lots of message queued up. Again you could ideally schedule out content for 6 months or even 1 year in advance.

When creating your email messages you don't have to use the entire article. You may just want to use the main points within the article and then discuss them in your email. You then lead your reader back to your website to read the full version of the original article.

When you want to send out additional messages just use the Broadcast feature. So we now have:

- Original article
- 1 Powerpoint Presentation
- 1 Video
- 1 PDF presentation from the slides
- Several blog posts scheduled
- Email messages loaded and ready to send out

WHERE TO USE YOUR NEW CONTENT

At this point you should have at least 6 different pieces of content that you can use. You don't have to use them all on your own website or blog.

Below is a list of other ways you can use this content:

1. Share your slides or PDF file to document sharing sites

2. Use one piece of this content to giveaway to new subscribers when they join your mailing list

3. Use within one of your emails to give as a gift or freebie

4. Use portions of your content as posts for your social media sites

5. Trim sentences to the correct length and use as Twitter posts

6. Share the images within your content on your Pinterest boards

CREATING REPORTS FROM SEVERAL ARTICLES OR BLOG POSTS

You can easily create short reports just by using the content of several articles and combining them into a report format. Of course you want to use articles that are relevant and informational.

Creating a 10 Page Quick Report

You can create a quick 10 page report by putting together 8 to 10 related articles. Combine them together in an easy to follow format. You may need to add one or two paragraphs so the sequence blends together. If you have longer articles you can use each one as a new section or chapter in your report.

Spruce up your report by making use of images and link out to other related information as necessary. If you are recommending specific products then don't forget to include your affiliate link in the report.

Add a contents page and a legal notice or disclaimer page. A general introduction is always a nice touch and allows you to add your own contact and website information. To expand your report further end the report with a conclusion page. Don't forget to include your contact details, so your readers can find you!

A title page or book cover helps to add that professional touch to your report. You can use any of the Cover options inside Microsoft Word. Or you could use a site like Fiverr and have someone create one for $5.

To add more professionalism to your report add a header and footer section along with page numbering. When you are happy with your report save it as a PDF file and your report is ready to go.

Where to Use Your New Report

1. Use as a giveaway to build your list
2. Use in a Giveaway Event, also to build your list
3. Sell it on your site or via an affiliate program
4. Create an Audio version of your report as an MP3

5. Give as a gift when people Like your page on Facebook

6. Use as a bonus to another product you have created

7. Use as a bonus on similar products you promoting as an affiliate

8. Use the content to run a webinar or Google+ Hangout

9. Give it to your affiliates and allow them to rebrand it with their affiliate link

REPURPOSING YOUR REPORT

We have looked at several ways to reuse or repurpose an article. Now let's look at larger quantities of content such as reports. How can you repurpose this type of material?

Once your report is written it is time to start thinking about how you can make use of this content again and again. Let's start by keeping the report as one product and seeing what we can do with it.

- Record an audio version of it and turn it into an MP3
- Create a Podcast from the content
- Take the highlights of the report and create PowerPoint slides, as we did with the article earlier in this report
- Share your report on document sharing sites
- Create a printed version of your report. You can easily do this on sites such as Lulu or CreateSpace

- Seek out professional magazines in your niche and try and get your report published as a featured article or story

Now we will start to chop up your report and see how we can use it. First, if you haven't used the individual articles that you used to create the report you can easily break down the content again. Use this segmented content as blog posts and email messages.

Other ideas for breaking down the content and repurposing include:

1. Creating a short term membership site
2. Setting up an email course and delivering sections via your autoresponder
3. Creating a coaching program with the content
4. Create courses to sell on sites such as Udemy or from your own site
5. Create a shorter version of this report and use to build your list or to giveaway to entice people to buy the full version

When chopping up the content the easiest way is to do it chapter by chapter. You could then create short videos for each new chapter. This will give you PowerPoint slides as well as videos to use.

So we now have the following from our Report:

- Several smaller articles
- Blog posts ready to publish
- PowerPoint slides
- Several short videos
- PDF presentation from the slides
- Professionally printed version of the report
- Content to use as a Bonus
- Content to give to affiliates to help sell other products
- Magazine content
- Membership content
- Ecourse content
- Coaching content
- Podcast content
- Audio versions
- Social Media content

OTHER IDEAS FOR REPURPOSING YOUR CONTENT

By now you should be seeing some of the possibilities of just how you can repurpose your content. Really the only limit is that of your imagination! Let's take a look at some additional ways to make good use of your content.

The ideas listed below will require that you change your content in order to make the best use of them.

Press Releases

This is a great way to reuse an article but it will include rewriting parts of the content as well. When writing a press release you do not want your release to be a sales pitch. Instead it needs to provide news.

When writing your press release it is perfectly acceptable to use strong words and always write in the active voice. This brings your press release to life and engages the reader immediately. Keep your press release fairly short and make it concise. The following are some great topic ideas for creating your press release.

- Announcing a new feature or product
- Hosting or participating in an event
- Sharing results from a survey
- Announcing any new changes in your business

Guest Post Material

You can use any of your articles and reports and use them for guest post material. When it comes to writing a guest post most blog owners require that you use original content that hasn't been published anywhere else.

This can be easily done by taking several of your articles and then rewriting them into one new guest post. Just take all the main points from each article and combine them. Include a new image and a link back to your main blog and your guest post is written.

You will have created a new original article without having to do a ton of research. Repeat this process as many times as possible so you can publish lots of guest posts on related websites. This helps your business by giving you additional exposure, back links and traffic back to your own site.

Research & Outline Material

With this method you are simply going to take the basic article or report and expand on it. This method is perfect for using with PLR content to expand it and make it unique to your own site.

PLR content is great for using as an outline for a new article, report or to create your own products with. Just use the base material and then perform some additional research to find more content.

For example say your PLR content is about dieting. Look for health related news and sites to see what new developments or trends are happening. Then include these in your report or product.

This allows you to take your dieting material and turn it into a highly relevant product. Think about when Acai Berries were popular or right now with the Juicing niche. By doing this you are also finding a target market at the same time. Your product will be targeted to those people looking to buy the latest diet trend. This in turn will help you get more sales once your product is released.

Mind Maps

People love visual aids and depending upon your niche and the content you can easily create a Mind map with your content. There are several Mindmaps software available, just do an internet search and download a program. Some of these will be paid software but you can still download free ones as well.

Social Media Content

We wanted to expand on using your content for social media. Today social media is becoming a huge factor for anyone who wants to have an online presence. The downside to using social media is that you need to add content regularly. Once you stop posting people will forget who you are.

You can reuse any of your articles or blog posts and turn them into social media content. Simply take a paragraph or two from each blog post and post it to your social sites. Make sure you add images as this will encourage people to share your content.

With Facebook marketing you can schedule content on your Fan Pages in advance. Try to add a heading that is a little controversial as this will help attract attention to your posts. You can also use a program such as Paint dot net and add a few words with the text feature.

For Twitter reuse your content by condensing sentences so that they ask questions or make comments. Short and sweet will work effectively here and you can schedule Tweets with programs such as Buffer and Hootsuite.

Don't forget to add images and graphics to your content and then post your images to Pinterest.

Using Your Content in Forums

Another way to reuse your content is by using the content to answer questions in forums and to answer questions left on your blog or on your social pages. If you are answering questions on sites such as Yahoo Answers then you can leave longer replies. Quora is a great question and answer site that you can use to build up your branding and showcase your expertise.

On other sites just leave a short paragraph and then suggest to the reader to read the rest of your article on your website.

When joining any type of forum always read the guidelines and abide by them. Showing your credibility on a forum can provide you with tons of exposure, but this method does take time to build upon. You definitely don't want to rush in and start dropping links and sales pitches all over the place.

Instead you want to join in various discussions and help people by answering questions and offering advice. In time you will become known as an expert in your niche. Use your article content to draft informative replies to questions. You may even be able to offer one of your free reports to members.

QUICK REWRITING TIPS

While we have mainly discussed reusing your content in this report we also wanted to give you a few rewriting tips. Again these tips apply to any type of content but are particularly useful when it comes to customizing PLR content.

When changing content one of the easiest ways to make your content different is by changing up some of the words. This is easy to do in Word or Open Office. Just highlight the word you would like to change and then right click your mouse. Choose Synonyms and a new list will appear. Make your selection and your choice is automatically placed into the content. Use the Thesaurus to find additional word replacements for your content.

Adding your personality to any piece of content will immediately render it as *'your content'*. While you do not need to rewrite the entire article or report you should add a couple of additional paragraphs.

The easiest way to do this is to add an introductory paragraph or opening to the content. This can be interspersed with additional thoughts and comments you have throughout the entire article. End with a closing paragraph and you have just customized your content to you and to your niche.

Content Curation Techniques and Tips

You can apply basic content curation methods to any of your current content. With content curation you are basically adding your opinion on a particular topic. Plus you reference other outside sources.

This is similar to the method we suggested above by adding your personality into any piece of content.

Use your basic article and then do a quick online search and look for current news articles on the same topic. You then add your take to the article and link to related news articles, again leaving your opinion. This will help expand your content and could create a certain amount of social interaction. This is very true if your content is controversial. Remember people love to leave their opinions not just on social sites but on your blog too.

CREATING A SALES FUNNEL
WITH YOUR CONTENT

If you intend to sell your own products from your website you should have a sales funnel in place. A sales funnel is basically a way to take interested people and entice them to purchase one or more of your products.

Here's how you can create a profitable sales funnel.

1. Use your available content to write a free report or create a free video which you can give away

2. Once someone downloads your free report they are taken to a One Time Offer

3. If they do not take your offer they are placed onto a Free List which you have set up inside your autoresponder account

4. If they accept your offer they are placed onto your Buyers List

5. You now have two lists which you can email on a regular basis Of course your next question is:

"What do I mail my list?"

You can do various things here:

Create additional reports which you can give to your list. Inside these reports would be your affiliate links to products which you are recommending. When someone buys through your link you make a commission.

Use content which you already have and split it up into short emails, as we mentioned in an earlier section. Then simply preload this content into each list. Always make sure that the content you are loading is relevant to your main free report or giveaway that you offered. Try to build upon that content by offering more advice and information interspersed with helpful offers.

As soon as someone from your free list makes a purchase you want to have them automatically placed onto your Buyers List. This can be achieved by using the automation rules inside your autoresponder account.

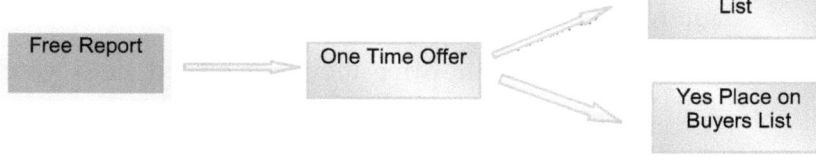

Now you have the basic outline of a sales funnel which you can put into place to increase your income and build your mailing list. All achieved by reusing content in different ways.

So far we have now repurposed our content by: Turning an article into:

- Powerpoint Presentation
- Video
- PDF presentation from the slides
- Several blog posts scheduled
- Email messages loaded and ready to send out
- Combined several articles into a quick short report

Which we then used as:

- Content to use as a Bonus
- Content to give to affiliates to help sell other products
- Professionally printed version of the report
- Magazine content
- Membership content
- Ecourse content
- Coaching content
- Podcast content
- Audio versions

We then chopped up the report to create:

- Blog posts ready to publish
- PowerPoint slides
- Several short videos
- PDF presentation from the slides
- Social Media content

All of these things can be done from existing content that you have sitting on your hard drive, or from PLR material or packages that you have recently purchased and done nothing with.

BUILDING WEB 2.0 PROPERTIES

Now that you have existing content in many different forms you want to use it to help increase your traffic and find prospects for your products or services. An excellent way to do this is by building out Web 2.0 properties. These are additional sites that can all link back to your main site or be used to build your email list or fan pages.

Web 2.0 sites are sites such as:

- Blogger
- Wordpress.com
- Hub Pages
- Squidoo Lenses
- Tumblr
- Weebly

Simply choose one or two and create related pages for your niche. If your main site is about fitness and exercise then create pages in specific niches such as losing 10 pounds quickly, how to start a juicing diet or exercising with kettlebells.

Use your repurposed content including blog posts, slides and videos as content for these sites. You can quickly create several new sites in one day or less using this method.

CREATING LANDING/SQUEEZE PAGES

A landing or squeeze page is a specific page that has one purpose only – to get a person onto your mailing list. To entice people to sign up to your list you normally give them something in return for parting with their email address. This can be your newly created report, your slide sharing document or one of your videos. It doesn't have to be lengthy, it does need to be relevant and offer quality information.

Here's an example of a landing page:

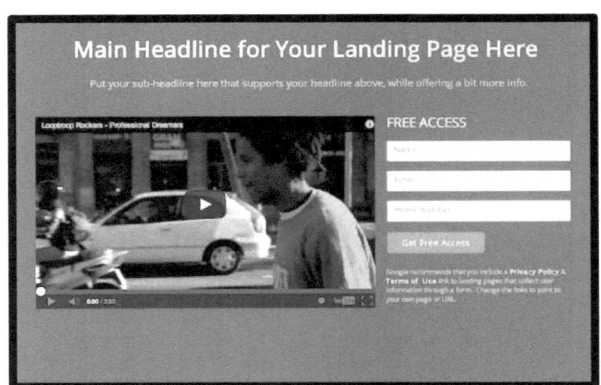

You would use your new content as the gift. Landing pages can have videos on them as shown above, or they can have bulleted lists highlighting the features and benefits of what you have to offer.

CREATING VIDEOS WITH YOUR CONTENT

Just the thought of creating videos can be overwhelming and immediately has your mind raising a red flag. Creating a basic video is not that difficult at all. Most older computers come with Windows Movie Maker and this is perfect for creating a video. Windows 7 and 8 may not include this software but you can download it online.

Your first step is to create a PowerPoint presentation with your content, as described earlier. You then save your presentation as JPEG files. Your next step is to open Windows Movie Maker and import your JPEG files. You drag each file down into your story board and add effects and a sound track or voice over, if using.

When you are satisfied with your movie you then save it as a movie file and then upload this to your YouTube account.

BEST PRACTICES FOR REPURPOSING YOUR CONTENT

Use the following tips as a guideline when repurposing any type of content.

1. Chop up and break down longer content into shorter snippets

2. Post smaller chunks as blog posts and use for autoresponder messages

3. Take these smaller chunks and then condensing them even further and use as content on your social media sites

4. Use the main highlights, tips and pointers to write Tweets

5. Add an introductory paragraph

6. Add a conclusion

7. Create PowerPoint slides and turn them into presentations or magazine style books by saving as a PDF

8. Use your PowerPoint slides and turn into videos

9. Add audio and/or music to your slides and videos

10. Add images and graphics to your content

11. Combine 8 to 10 articles and create ready to go reports

12. Share your content on Document Sharing sites

13. Create free giveaway reports

14. Create reports that you can sell from your website

15. Create reports for your affiliates, embed with their affiliate links

16. Use your content to build Web 2.0 properties which link back to your main site

WHY REPURPOSE YOUR CONTENT?

There are many benefits from taking the time to repurpose your content. At first you may find this to be a lengthy process. As you become accustomed to using these methods you will find that the process is fairly quick.

Some of the main benefits include:

- Stops you from being a slave to your blog, you can free up time by scheduling out posts in advance.

- Saves you money as you will not have to constantly buy new content each time you want to add new material to your site. You will save enough money that you can afford to purchase better quality content and you will know how to reuse it over and over again.

- Provides you with GREAT value for your money, you are only buying once and can reuse your content countless times!

- Gives you more exposure across multiple platforms and helps brand both you as an expert and your business.
- Your new repurposed content gives you back links for your site. Great for SEO purposes and helps you rank higher in the search engines.

CONCLUSION

By now the benefits of repurposing should be extremely clear to you. Using the methods described within this eBook will allow you to really get the biggest bang for your buck!

While we have discussed several repurposing methods you do not have to use all of them each time. Find the ones that you enjoy doing and those which will offer the best benefits for your business model and then simply repeat this process multiple times.

You now have no excuses for not using any content which has been taking up space on your hard drive over the last few months or longer. Why not create two new folders for all the content you wish to reuse. Label one: Content to Use and label the second: Repurposed Content and then challenge yourself to see how quickly you can fill up the second folder!

All of the methods outlined in this eBook apply to any type of content that you have created yourself. If you have purchased articles and reports ensure that you have the correct license so that you can edit, rip apart and reuse the material in any way you see fit. This is the benefit of using PLR content, as most PLR producers allow you to edit and reuse their content. Always check the license or read me file if you are in doubt, or contact the provider via email.

Printed by Libri Plureos GmbH in Hamburg,
Germany